Todd Gray

THE MINT PRESS

The Essence of EXETER

The Essence of EXETER

Patron: The Express & Echo

Express&Echo 1904 - 2004
CENTE&ENARY
BRINGING THE NEWS TO EXETER & THE HEART OF DEVON FOR 100 YEARS

First published in Great Britain by The Mint Press, 2004

ISBN 1-903356-38-5

Cataloguing in Publication Data
CIP record for this title is available from the British Library

The Mint Press
18 The Mint
Exeter, Devon
England EX4 3BL

Page design and layout by Topics – The Creative Partnership, Exeter.
Cover design by Delphine Jones.

Printed and bound in Great Britain
by Brightsea Press Ltd, Exeter

Acknowledgements

I would like to thank Gillian Selley who provided Soyer's recipe for Exeter Pudding and I am very grateful to John Allan, Stuart Blaylock, Richard Parker, Margery Rowe and Dr Mark Stoyle for their comments which have considerably improved this book. Any and all remaining mistakes are of course my own. I would also like to thank Delphine Jones for her splendid cover and the Express and Echo for acting as patron.

Contents

The Essence of

EXETER

E xeter has dominated its region for more than two thousand years. It is not surprising that a city that was the principal focus for commerce, culture, politics, tourism, education and religion became the region's capital. It has long been accepted that the Romans established Exeter in about 55 AD but archaeological exploration is now revealing that there was an Iron Age setlement here before the legionaries established Isca, their fortress at the western edge of Roman Britain. Through the medieval period until the early 1700s Exeter was one of the most prosperous cities in England after becoming a centre for a cloth industry. It commanded a large region and both of its nearest rivals, Bristol at the far end of yet another county and Plymouth at the further south-west tip of Devon, were situated a considerable distance away. The city has always been rebuilt and prospered despite the traumas of two Viking invasions in 876 and 1003, two long sieges in the civil war between 1642 and 1645, and the blitz of the second world war in 1942. The population today, of some 112,000, is the largest there has ever been and Exeter remains the region's capital more than two thousand years after being established.

Over the centuries Exeter has been shaped by a great number of influences with the result that it has a distinct character with a number of features unique

A gentleman at Mol's Coffee House, painted as remembered by Mr Tucker in the mid nineteenth century.

Opposite:
One of the city's Roman mosaics which escaped destruction unlike others found in the nineteenth century.

5

One of the city's Victorian celebrations of the fifth of November.

to it. The city has buildings with unusual histories such as the timber-framed building commonly known as Mol's in Cathedral Close. It may well be unique in that during the long Georgian period, from the 1720s until the 1830s, it was a coffee house which served the well-to-do throughout the region and was a centre for the gathering of business news and gossip. Most interesting of all, it was owned and run only by women: seven women were in charge of the coffee house over the course of more than a century. The city also once had a number of celebration days particular to it. Following the Prayer Book Rebellion in 1549 Exeter celebrated August 8 as 'Jesus Day' with public lectures. The celebrations for 5th November were the largest in the county until the late nineteenth century[1]. Cathedral Yard was the location for popular occasions, such as in 1688 during the last few chaotic months of the reign of James II, but the city was famous for its bonfires, the rolling of tar barrels, fireworks and the general level of

---

[1] Todd Gray, *Exeter Unveiled* (Exeter, 2003),65-7.

mayhem caused by the thousands of local people celebrating Bonfire Night. Like many other places in the country the city observed the walking of parish boundaries: in Exeter it was called 'Possessioning Day' and locals shouted 'Hip! Hip! Hurrah!' as they wandered through their parishes on Ascension Day (ten days before Whitsunday). However, during the week before young boys terrorised other inhabitants by blocking watercourses in the streets and demanding tolls for safe passage. Then on Possessioning Day itself gangs of young lads fought other boys over parish boundaries. In 1865 Charles Dickens wrote about Exeter's day and called it 'Processioning Day'.[2] The parish of Allhallows-on-the-Walls may have been the last parish to celebrate this 'scramble' but by the 1890s it was just a memory. In 1893 it was remembered that men, as well as boys, participated.[3]

Incidentally, these bouts gave rise to Exeter's unique name for its football team: since the early 1900s they have been known as the Grecians but the name goes back at least to the 1690s when it applied to the lads from the parish of St Sidwell, which is outside the eastern walls of the city, on Possessioning Day. Curiously, boys from outside the western walls of the city, in the parish of St Thomas, then had the nickname of the 'Algerines'. By the early eighteenth century it appears as though Grecians, or Greeks, became a general term for residents of the parish of St Sidwell.[4] It is not known how either the Grecians or the Algerines acquired their names but the city's footballers, whose grounds are based in St Sidwell parish, took the name of the Grecians when a name was looked for in 1908.[5] Only Lammas Fair is still observed in the city: the Fair was traditionally held on 1 August and refers to the 'loaf mass' when the first fruits of the harvest season were celebrated as a symbolic loaf of bread.[6]

Posessioning Day as portrayed by George Townsend in the nineteenth century. The week before was frantic: young boys fought each other over parish borders and shouted amongst other things 'Sally up! Sally up!' and 'Oller boys! Oller boys!' They also dammed waterways and demanded pennies from passing strangers with threats of splashing. The artist noted

"this healthful exhilarating exhibition of muscular christening was to be seen for about a week before Possessioning Day in the first half of the century chasing and running away with flourishing of sticks and shouts of defiance were the usual characteristics, but sometimes real fighting. Sometimes also a shower from overhead changed the ardour of the combatants. Instruction in the three R's and School Board have doubtlessly contributed to the abolition of parish fighting."

[2] Charles Dickens, *All the year round*, October 28, 1865, page 320.

[3] A 'Ascension-Day Scramble at Allhallows-on the- wall', *The Western Times*, 12 May 1893.

[4] Andrew Brice, *The Mobiad*, (1770), 75.

[5] *Express and Echo*, 25 9 1951; 'Those without the West Gate whom they call the Algerines and those of St Sidwell whom they call the Grecians...' DRO, 73/15, fo. 134 cited by Mark Stoyle, *Loyalty and Locality* (Exeter, 1994), 109.

[6] Ronald Hutton, *The Rise and Fall of Merry England, the ritual year 1400–1700* (Oxford, 1994), 44; David Cressy, *Bonfires and Bells* (1989), 28.

Symbols of EXETER

It would be difficult to choose a symbol for Exeter because of its rich and varied history. The view of the cathedral from the west must be the most recognizable, with the West Front and the two great towers, but there are several others which are also particularly interesting as they reflect the rich culture of Exeter. The gate to Rougemont Castle, the front of the Guildhall or the City Arms are also possible candidates. John Hooker's late sixteenth-century map is one of the best known images of Exeter. The `lucky horseshoe' of Harry Hems, the celebrated Victorian artisan, must be one of the

Top Right: *The West Front of the Cathedra.l*
Above: *The Norman Gate to Rougemont Castle, and The Guildhall, with its late sixteenth-century porch.*
Right: *John Hooker's map of Elizabethan Exeter.*

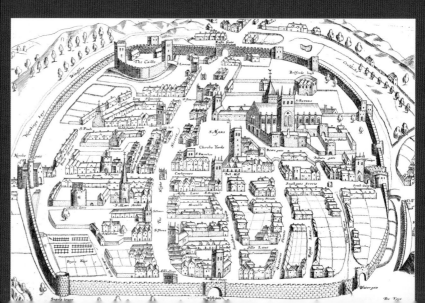

Top: *Harry Hems' Lucky Horseshoe, Longbrook Street.*
Left: *Mathew the Miller, Church of St Mary Steps.*
Above: *The Phoenix, 1957, in Princesshay.*
Below right: *Gerald the Giraffe, in the Royal Albert Memorial Museum.*

most positive images of the city. Hems wrote that he found his horseshoe upon arriving at Exeter and then placed it high on his building in Longbrook Street, where it can still be seen today, as a totem to Hems' later success. There is also the post-war representation of the Phoenix, symbol of Exeter's rebirth after the destruction of the second world war, which is also an iconic image. The figure of Mathew the Miller, which for centuries has announced the passing hours at the church of St Mary Steps, is one of the most popular figures in the city. Even more so is probably Gerald the Giraffe; this bull Masai has been situated in the Royal Albert Memorial Museum since 1919 and in that time has delighted many thousands of children. To many he is probably the face of Exeter.

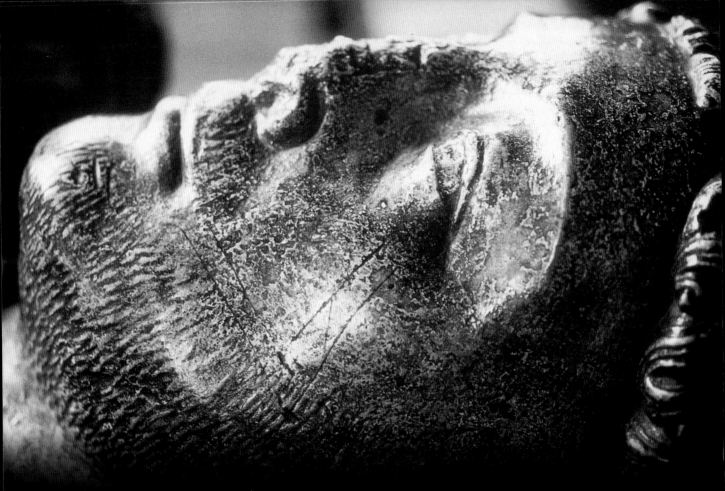

The medieval effigy of Bishop Bronscombe in the cathedral.

Exeter Cathedral's medieval elephant.

But there are others: in the cathedral lies the well-known late medieval effigy of Bishop Bronescombe. He must rank as one of Exeter's chief worthies. The cathedral's medieval carved elephant is another favourite. Finally, the medieval wooden statue of St Peter is particularly interesting: it stood overlooking the Carfax for some six centuries through the Reformation and the Civil War until the 1980s. It remains one of the city's greatest treasures and an apt symbol of success and endurance.

Pride in the city has resulted in its name being taken across the world. There are eighteen others comprising one in Ontario in Canada, three in Australia (in South

Inset: Detail from The Cap showing the Exeter Coat of Arms.
Above: When Exeter hosted the Great Exhibition of 1850 it still had its clock on St John's church tower in Fore Street with its golden dial expressing Exeter Time and silver one showing London Time.

St Peter, who stood at the Carfax for centuries and now rests in the Royal Albert Memorial Musem.

Australia, New South Wales and Tasmania) and fourteen in the United States (in California, Illinois, Maine, Missouri, Nebraska, New Hampshire, New York, Pennsylvania, Rhode Island and Wisconsin).

It was probably independence of spirit that was behind the decision of the city in the 1840s not to capitulate to London by adopting its time zone: the city used London time but maintained a separate Exeter time. For some seven years a clock on Fore Street showed both times, with separate minute hands distinguishing between London and Exeter time. [7]

Returning the compliment: Pennsylvania in Exeter was named after the American state and this local banknote depicts William Penn and his famous undertaking with native Americans.

[7] Clive Ponsford, *Time in Exeter* (1978), 11, 14.

11

TOPOGRAPHY

I n some ways it is easy to understand the choice of land which became Exeter. This flattish area along the ridge of high ground at the most convenient crossing point of the river Exe would have appealed to the Romans as a defensive site. Hopefully archaeology will reveal more in the next few years about those who lived in Exeter in the years before them. The street layout is more straightforward than it might be because there has been comparatively little change, particularly in relation to say Plymouth. The High Street is the oldest thoroughfare and was a prehistoric trackway leading to a ford over the river. It follows the ancient ridge-way which came in from Sidwell Street and disappears into Fore Street.[8] The city was dissected only by one other road north to south (the current North and South Streets) and the outward points of these four streets were their ancient gates and the great wall which enclosed the entire city. At the meeting point of High, Fore, South and North Streets is the Carfax. The city shares this place name, from the Middle English or Old French meaning the crossways of four streets, only with Oxford and the Sussex town of Horsham. This was the central gathering point of the city, where all the traffic of the city met and one of the places where proclamations were read.

Exeter has been defined by three areas of independent jurisdictions: from the 1060s the Crown, or the Duchy of Cornwall, has held the precincts of Rougemont Castle, the established church has held sway in the Cathedral Close and Yard and finally the great mass of land in the south east of the city of what is now Princesshay,

[8] W.G. Hoskins, *Two Thousand Years in Exeter* (Exeter, 1960), 142; C.G.Henderson, 'The City of Exeter from AD 50 to the early nineteenth century', in Roger Kain and William Ravenhill, *Historical Atlas of South-West England* (Exeter, 1999), 482.

was formerly a house of the Black Friars and later included the town house of the earls of Bedford and finally Bedford Circus, probably the finest example of Georgian architecture in the city. These three areas operated independently of the city authorities. Exeter also has some unusual streets: Parliament Street has been cited as the narrowest in England at 24 inches wide at ground level.[9] At the roofline the distance is less: at one point the buildings nearly meet one another. The derivation of the name is uncertain but it was given it shortly after 1828. One erroneous story was that it was named after a parliament called by Edward I who was in Exeter in 1285 but more recently it has been suggested that it was derived from the Reform Bill of 1832.[10] A survey of English cities has not revealed a narrower street[11] but that in the world is probably in Italy.[12] Another unusual thoroughfare is Bridge Street, perhaps the only one in the country built on top of a redundant bridge. Exeter also has an unusual custom, going back to at least the early 1200s, in removing the word saint from streets named after nearby churches such as Mary Arches, Paul and Sidwell Streets.

Exeter has always been a red city, so much so that in 1805 Robert Southey, the celebrated poet, imagined that the early British inhabitants, many hundreds of years before him, called it 'The Red City'.[14] The local stone, which ranges from red to purplish grey, was used for the city gates, its Roman walls and such prominent buildings as the Guildhall and all of the twenty medieval parish churches. Even part of the cathedral was constructed of it,

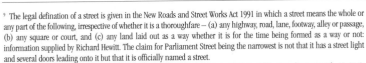

The remains of the Roman Bath House, situated to the west of the West Front of the cathedral, rediscovered and then covered over in the early 1970s.

---

[9] The legal defination of a street is given in the New Roads and Street Works Act 1991 in which a street means the whole or any part of the following, irrespective of whether it is a thoroughfare – (a) any highway, road, lane, footway, alley or passage, (b) any square or court, and (c) any land laid out as a way whether it is for the time being formed as a way or not: information supplied by Richard Hewitt. The claim for Parliament Street being the narrowest is not that it has a street light and several doors leading onto it but that it is officially named a street.

[10] *The Guiness Book of Records* (London 16th edn, 1969); *Exeter Literacy and General Directory* (Exeter, 1828), *19*; W. G. Hoskins, *Two Thousand Years in Exeter* (Exeter, 1960), 146.

[11] Over sixty cities and towns in England were asked in the spring of 2004: replies were made by staff of the councils of Bristol, Nottingham, Norwich, Leeds, Cambridge, Winchester, Worcester, Coventry, Kingston Upon Hull, Guildford, Southampton, Truro and Leicester that they did not have a narrower street. An inquiry was also placed in Notes & Queries in *The Guardian*, 5th May 1905, supplement, page 18 and two answers on the 19th of the month refered to alleys in general and to Dog Loup in Staithes, Yorkshire, in particular. It is only 15 inches in width but is not termed as a 'street'. There are also other alleys and passageways narrower than Parliament Street but which are not called streets.

[12] It appears this is the village of Ripatransone in Italy at 16.9 inches: information supplied by the *Guinness World Records*.

[13] *Two Thousand Years in Exeter*, 146.

[14] Todd Gray (ed.) *Exeter The Travellers Tales* (Exeter, 2000) 102.

although finer white stone was brought in to face the building. The city is coloured a patchwork of red in spite of brick not being used until comparatively recently. Some nineteenth-century suburbs, such as Newtown, were built of brick but the centre of the city clothed itself in red through the use of local quarries. Even the name of the castle, Rougemont – the red hill, is derived from this building material and an examination of the city underfoot, in its underground passages, shows that red stone line the city's medieval water courses. The city has always been red from top to bottom.

It is not surprising that in such an ancient city there are buildings with elements which date back two thousand years. The city walls stand on Roman foundations and sections contain identifiable Roman work.[15] There is a Roman tile in the church of St Martin (as well as in the ruins of St George's Church and

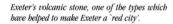
Exeter's volcanic stone, one of the types which have helped to make Exeter a `red city'.

---

[15] Mark Stoyle, *Circled with Stone* (Exeter, 2003), 8–12.

A view of the South Gate by Thomas Rowlandson, by 1820. These buildings were built following the destruction outside the city walls during the Civil War and perhaps typify the type of style for which Exeter is associated with.

Plaster work at the Custom House.

in the Chapter House at the Cathedral), until recently a Saxon cross stood in front of St Nicholas Priory and a Norman font can still be seen in the church of St Mary Steps. Evidence of Saxon masonry can be seen in the churches of St Martin and St Olave. One of the oldest standing buildings in the region is St Nicholas Priory, founded in the 1080s, with its impressive Norman undercroft. The gatehouse at Rougemont Castle is recognised as the country's earliest standing castle building, built in about 1069, and Cathedral Close has the finest collection of medieval buildings in the region. The city has an overlay of buildings going back a thousand years with notable examples from the medieval, Elizabethan, Georgian and Victorian periods. This is in spite of two periods of great devastation during the Civil War in the 1640s and bombing by the Luftwaffe in 1942 which caused the destruction of many hundreds of buildings. The latter disaster was followed by a period of rebuilding in the 1950s and 1960s and it was from this era that a gradual realisation of the city's architectural treasures arose: the move in 1961 of a medieval house from impending demolition is the visible reminder of this consciousness. Devon is a county known for its ornamental plasterwork of the seventeenth century and in Exeter there are some of the best examples: for instance, the Custom House has spectacular ceilings designed by John Abbott in 1680 and there are other spectacular ones at the Royal Albert Memorial Museum and St Nicholas Priory.

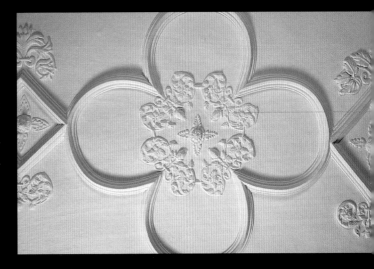

Equally impressive is the ceiling at St Nicholas Priory.

Exeter can distinguish itself by a large number of `hayes' within and around the city walls. `Haye' is an Old English word for an enclosure and there were at least ten of them - Calendar hay, Southern hay, Northern hay, Bon hay, Friern hay, Shil hay, Tric hay, Dodde hay, Friar's hay and Mill hay - which were joined by Princesshay in 1949. In the early seventeenth century the city authorities reorganised Northernhay as a `pleasant walk' for local people and wooden benches were set out. On this basis it has been acknowledged as the country's first public park[16] but it is less known that a generation before this the city authorities planted trees throughout Exeter to enhance public areas (`to the great comfort of the viewers').[17]

From at least the sixteenth century, and into the eighteenth, local people and visitors compared Exeter favourably with London and was called by them the region's `Emporium', the `Metropolis' or `Metropole of the West' and the `London of the West'. It had become the regional centre of commerce, culture, education, religion, politics and tourism.

[16] Todd Gray, 'Their Idols of Worship', 28 in Stephen Pugsley, *Devon Gardens, an Historical survey* (Stroud, 1994).
[17] Walter J. Harte (ed.), *The Description of the Citie of Excester* (Devon & Cornwall Record Society, 1919), Part II, 3.

COMMERCE

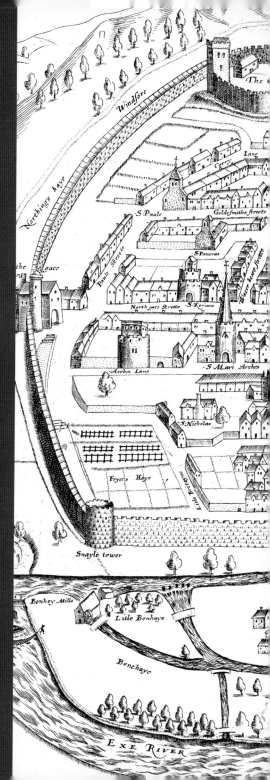

Through the medieval period Exeter was the `Head Port' for customs; this meant that it had priority in what was the largest royal customs jurisdiction. The hall for the medieval guild of the Weavers, Tuckers and Shearmen, now known as Tuckers Hall, is the county's most prominent survivor from the glory days of the `Golden Fleece' – it was the woollen cloth trade in the region which made the city wealthy.[18] The guild is also still in existence, an unusual survivor in the country. The city's Custom House is the most impressive in the region and still dominates the quay, more than 300 years after it was built. From it one can see the city's canal, the first lock canal created in the country. The river Exe was blocked during the fourteenth century but it was not until after the Reformation, in the 1530s, that the city authorities began to plan a canal to link Exeter the four miles to Topsham, their ancient outlet to the sea. The design used pairs of sluices which created pound locks and the canal opened in the mid 1560s.[19] The canal still operates.

John Hooker's late sixteenth-century map: in this period the city's wealth was tied to the cloth trade.

[18] Robert Newton, *Eighteenth Century Exeter* (Exeter, 1984), 25.
[19] E.A.G. Clark, *The Ports of the Exe Estuary, 1660 – 1860* (Exeter, 1968 edn), 28-9.

One traveller described the city during its heyday

'*Exeter is a town very well built the streets are well pitched, spacious noble streets, and a vast trade is carried on; as Norwich is for copes, calamanco and damask so this is for serges - there is an incredible quantity of them made and sold in the town; their market day is Friday which supplies with all things like a fair almost; the markets for meat, fowl, fish, garden things, and the dairy produce takes up 3 whole streets besides the large Market house set on stone pillars, which runs a great length, on which they lay their packs of serges, just by it is another walk within pillars, which is for the yarn. The whole town and county is employed for at least 20 mile round in spinning, weaving, dressing and scouring, fulling and drying of the serges. It turns the most money in a week of anything in England. One week with another there is £10,000 paid in ready money, sometimes £15,000,*'

CELIA FIENNES, 1698.

19

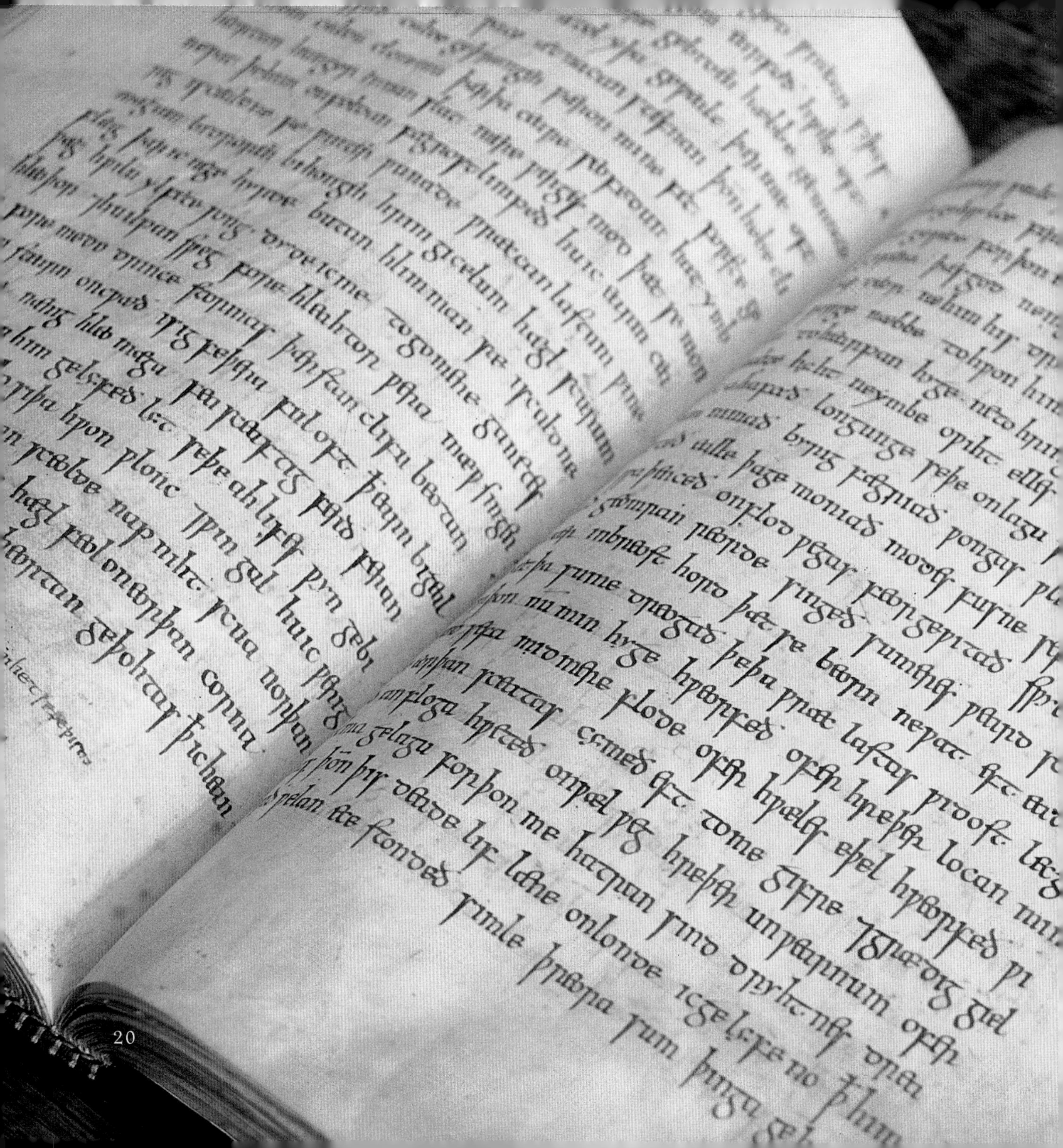

CULTURE

The city's Anglo Saxon Book of Poetry, sometimes known as the Exeter Riddle Book, is one of the country's greatest literary treasures: this tenth-century manuscript has been called `one of the greatest surviving monuments of Anglo-Saxon literature'.[20] A thousand years after being written it still remains in Exeter. The city has a tradition of keeping its ancient manuscripts: John Hooker, the Elizabethan Chamberlain, collected and organised the city's documents, ancient even then, because, he wrote, of his sense of duty and love for his native Exeter. For hundreds of years, until living memory, they were kept at the Guildhall and now comprise the greatest collection of civic manuscripts outside London.

Newspapers were printed here far earlier than most British cities: the first papers outside London were published in 1701 and it is thought Exeter had its own newspaper only three years later.[21] Today's local paper, *The Express & Echo*, is the inheritor of that tradition and has itself been running for one hundred years. It is the only one to have that title in the country. Georgian gentlemen gathered in the city to read local and national newspapers at Mol's Coffee House in Cathedral Close and they met in other public houses to form dozens of local societies. One such group on beekeeping was the first of its kind in the country

Above: *John Hooker.*
Left: *The Anglo-Saxon Book of Poetry.*

---

[20] Audrey Erskine, *'Library and Archives'*, 193, in Michael Swanton (ed.), *Exeter Cathedral – A Celebration* (Exeter, 1991).
[21] Harte, *Description*, Part II, 1-2.

21

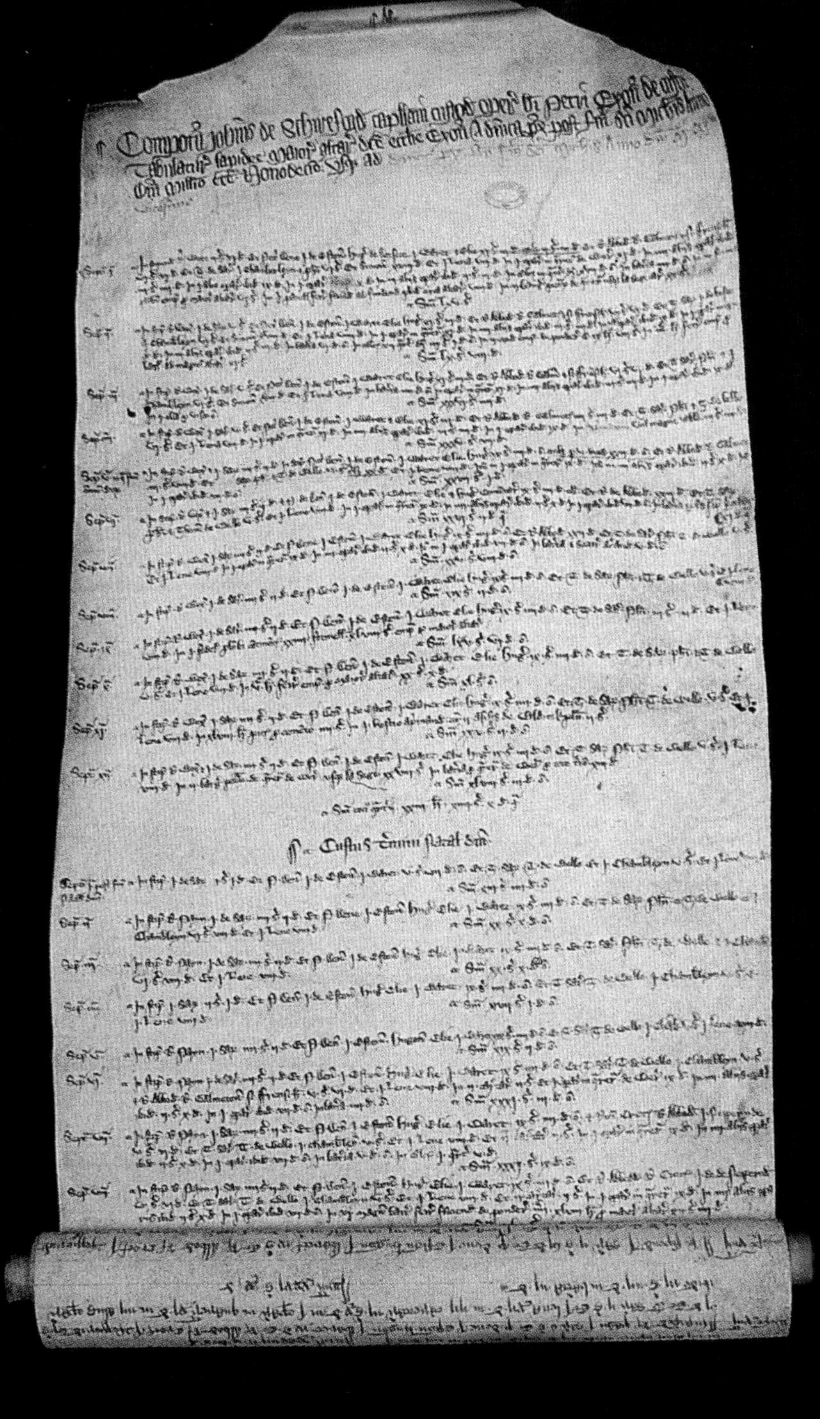

One of the many documents from the city's exceptional collection, a medieval fabric roll.

I'm a strange creature, for I satisfy women,

a service to my neighbours! No one suffers

at my hand except for my slayer.

I grow very tall, erect in a bed,

I'm hairy underneath. From time to time

A beautiful girl, the brave daughter

of some churl dares to hold me,

grips my russet skin, robs me of my head

and puts me in the pantry. At once that girl

with plaited hair who has confined me

remembers our meeting. Her eye moistens.

in 1797 and in the Devon and Exeter Horticultural Society it has one of the oldest provincial societies of its kind. It was formed in 1829.[23] The city's theatres were well known and attracted many of the foremost actors of the day notably the great Shakespearian actor Edmund Kean in the early 1800s. He was later remembered walking the streets of Exeter dressed in his costumes, famously once as Richard III.[24] Georgian Exeter was captured in the Hogarthian portrait *The Mobiad* and Anthony Trollope later used the city in *He Knew He Was Right*. The latter used to visit Fanny Bird, a friend of his mother's, who lived in Cathedral Close. The Close was also the setting from which Bram Stoker had Jonathan Hawker leave for his

Andrew Brice, who started the printing of newspapers in Exeter. He also wrote a short, but what is thought to be the earliest, manuscript description of a Mummers' Play. (See over).

[23] John Caldwell, 'Some notes on the first British Beekeeping Society', DAT, LXXXVIII, 1956, 65.
[24] Hoskins, *Two Thousand Years*, 80: Newton, *Eighteenth Century Exeter*, 25.

23

The *Express and Echo* has been running for a hundred years, from a tradition of three hundred years of newsapers in Exeter. The city had one of the first newspapers in the country outside London.

ill-fated trip to Transylvania. William Makepeace Thackeray renamed Exeter in *Pendennis* as Chatteris, R. S. Hawker in *Sweet and Twenty* called it Northminster and Thomas Hardy named it Exonbury in *Jude the Obscure* and three other works.[25] Exeter does not have any well-known playwrights but it does have the earliest recorded Mummers' Play, written in 1738.[26]

The historic culture of the city was brought together by the Victorians when the City Fathers built the Royal Albert Memorial Museum in the 1860s: this treasure house has long been pre-eminent within the region. Its collections in

'Still queueing for papers' at the Express & Echo offices, 1949

At Christmas are (or at least very lately were) fellows wont to go about from House to House in Exeter a mumming; one of whom in a (borrowed) Holland shirt most gorgeously be-ribboned, over his waistcoat, &c flourishing a falchion, very valiantly entertaining the admiring spectators thus

Oh! Here comes I Saint George, a man of courage bold

And with my spear I winned three Crowns of Gold.

I slew the Dragon, and brought him to the Slaughter.

And by that very means I married Sabra, the beauteous

  King of Egypt's daughter.

Play music

Exeter Mummers' Play

[25] Robert Cooper, *The Literary Guide and Companion to Southern England* (Athens, Ohio, 1985), 287; Simon Tresize, *The West Country as a Literary Invention* (Exeter 2000), 45; Paul Wreyford, *A Literary Tour of Devon* (Newton Abbot, 1996), 60-2,
[26] Todd Gray, *Christmas in Devon* (Exeter 2000), 18.

archaeology, silver, costumes and textiles, woodwork and coins are exceptional within a national context but the World Culture Galleries, which include items brought back from the Pacific by Captain Cook, are of wide international significance.

The city has established ties with the history of English gardening with the great firm of John Veitch. In the nineteenth century it was to Exeter that the country looked for the importation of newly-discovered exotic plants from around in the world gathered by men sent abroad by this great local nursery: dozens of plants which gardeners take for granted today were introduced by Veitch and other nurseries which surrounded the city including that founded by Charles Sclater in about 1824 and that by William Lucombe (later Lucombe, Pince & Co) a hundred years before him in 1720. There were also the Ford brothers from the late eighteenth century.[27] It was from this great interest that we have the extraordinary Wysteria Walk in St Thomas, now in its third, or fourth, century. Many varieties of plants have been named after the city such as the cider apple Red Hill Crab (also called the Royal Wilding) found in St Thomas in the early eighteenth century. Others cultivated in the city include the variety of passion flower 'Exoniensis' in about 1860 and there are similar varieties of Acacia, Calceolaria, Cattleya, Escallonia, Fuchsia, Gesneria, Kniphofia, Naegelia, Nerine, Pinus, Rhododendron and Ulmus. Finally, Exeter is closely associated with the Lucombe Oak. This evergreen oak originated at William Lucombe's nursery in about 1763 and at least one of the original grafts can still be found in the campus of Exeter University.[28] Finally, there is even a dessert named after the city. In 1850, when Exeter hosted the national agricultural exhibition Alexis Benoît

Painted decoration in St Nicholas Priory, late sixteenth century. Among the subjects are cherubs and grotesques.

[27] Audrey le Leièvre, *To the nobility and gentry about to plant: nurseries and nurserymen',* in Stephen Pugsley (ed.), *Devon Gardens, an historical survey* (Stroud, 1994), 91-7.
[28] *The Magic Tree, Devon Garden Plants,* (Exeter, 1989), 83, 109-161; Gray, ' Their Idols of Worship', 37.

The Royal Albert Memorial Museum, treasure house of the city's ancient culture.

Soyer, the leading chef of his day, created `Exeter Pudding' but he kept the recipe secret. It was said at the time that `all the matrons of the ancient city were striving to obtain the recipe'.

'A Victorian Exonian.'

Recipe for Monsieur Soyer's Exeter Pudding, 1850

Put into a proper-sized basin ten ounces of fine bread crumbs, four ounces of sago, seven ounces of suet (chopped fine), six ounces of moist sugar, the grated peel of half a lemon, a quarter of a pint of rum, and four eggs. Stir for a few minutes with a spoon, add three more eggs, four tablespoons of clotted cream and mix well. It is then ready to fill the mould. Butter the mould well, put in a handful of breadcrumbs, shake the mould well until the greater part sticks to the butter and then throw out the remainder. Have ready six penny sponge cakes, two ounces of ratafias [either cake or biscuit flavoured with a cordial or liqueur of either almonds, peaches, apricots or cherries], and half a pound of raspberry or strawberry jam. Cover the bottom of the mould with a layer of the ratafias, cover them with a layer of the mixture, cut the sponge cakes lengthways, spread each piece thickly with some jam, place a layer in the mould, then a few ratafias afterwards, some mixture and so on until the mould is full, taking care that a layer of the mixture is on top of the pudding. It will take about forty minutes baking. For the sauce put in a small stew pan three tablespoons of currant jelly and two glasses of sherry, warm on the fire and pour over the pudding. Serve Hot.

Education

E xeter has a longstanding interest in education. There was a grammar school by the late twelfth century, but the development of higher education was impeded by the establishment of Exeter College in 1314 at Oxford which was intended for scholars from the West Country. Exeter University took a further five centuries to develop and began in 1855 when the School of Art was founded. Ten years later the Albert Memorial building was erected and comprised a School of Art, museum, library and other rooms. In the 1890s plans were made to reorganise, already supplemented by evening courses organised by the University of Cambridge and the Science and Art Department at South Kensington: from this came the Royal Albert Memorial College which lasted until 1922 when the University College of the South West of England was created. It had been located in Gandy Street (now the Arts Centre) since 1906 but moved in 1922 to its present site north of the city. In 1955 it received its charter and became the University of Exeter. In 1978 it joined with St Luke's College, founded in 1839 to train teachers for Church of England schools; it is, along with St Mark's at Chelsea, the first of its kind in Britain.[29] The city is also distinguished by Mrs Treadwin's Lace School, now No. 5 Cathedral Close. This was the only school established for workers in East Devon Lace; in the early 1800s adults were taught elements of good taste in design but the school later took pupils aged twelve to fourteen years old.[30] Exeter also has the cathedral library, almost 1,000 years old, and the Devon & Exeter Institution, the region's leading surviving private subscription library which was founded in the early 1800s and has one of the finest libraries in the South West.

Students at the University College of the South-West, early twentieth century, in Gandy Street.

[29] Hoskins, *Two Thousand Years in Exeter,* 34-5; Nicholas Orme, *Education in the West of England, 1066–1548* (Exeter, 1976), 42-57; B.W. Clapp, *The University of Exeter: A History* (Exeter, 1982), 1-12. *The Western Times,* 21 October 1854.
[30] Todd Gray, *Lost Devon; creation, change and destruction over 500 years* (Exeter, 2004), 15.

Religion

The cathedral has dominated the city for nearly a thousand years as the hub of a regional diocese that included Cornwall with Devon. It was not until the nineteenth century that Cornwall had its own diocese. The cathedral has also been the dominant religious building since the Norman Conquest. During the building of the early fourteenth century it was at the forefront of European design, an innovative piece of architecture by Thomas of Witney which made Exeter renowned throughout the continent. It is known for its great North and South Towers, the span of its vaulting and particularly for the West Front, one of two surviving examples of medieval figure sculptures in Britain which, along with Wells, accounts for ninety per cent of that left in the country. There are treasures inside including the misericords, the oldest set in England. These thirteenth-century wood carvings famously feature an elephant amongst a great number of other subjects. Another treasure is the Bishop's Throne, a grand piece of early fourteenth-century woodwork widely acknowledged as the most elaborate of its date in the country. It is possible to view the cathedral as a great institution of religious art filled with pieces from the medieval period up to the present day. The monuments to the dead include early medieval works to unusual representations, such as the native American featured on the Georgian memorial to

Left: *The Bishop's Throne*

General Simcoe, and to individuals with unusual names including Reverend Nutcombe Nutcombe of Nutcombe. Finally, one of its great features are the bells: there are fifteen (named Grandison, Cobthorne, Stafford, Old and Little Nine O'Clock, Jubilee, Thomas I & II, Birdall, Pennington, Purdue, Pongamouth, Fox, Doom and Peter). The latter is acknowledged as the oldest of its weight and the biggest of its age.[31]

Before the Reformation Exeter had a great number of monastic houses and was later remembered as 'Monktown'.[32] One of the survivors is St Nicholas Priory. This impression of a great religious centre was undoubtedly reinforced by the large number of parish churches, in stark contrast to Plymouth which had one church for the whole population until the seventeenth century. As many as thirty churches once a feature of the city have been lost: among these were St Mary Major which stood directly in front of the cathedral until it was pulled down in the early 1970s and a church built into the city walls (All Hallows) which was destroyed during the Civil War. The church of Holy Trinity was unusual in being attached to a city's gate and its gaol and St Petrock was entirely encircled by secular buildings - parishioners could only see the tower of their church from the outside. The church of St Olave is distinguished by being dedicated to a Viking king and martyr, a legacy of the Scandinavian influence on the city. Only eight of these churches have survived (Saints Martin, Mary Arches, Mary Steps, Olave, Pancras, Petrock, Stephen and Trinity) but even these, with their red stone, continue to make an impact. One of the most satisfying internal objects is a sculpture in the church of St Petrock by John Weston, who was working in the early eighteenth century. His relief of the Last Judgement can be cherished while the rush of traffic races by outside. His work was said to have 'all the grace and movement of the Italian Renaissance'.[33]

The other statue of St Peter, above the West Front, 1985.

Left: *One of the ancient wooden doors in the city; This one is at Number 10-11 in the close.*

[31] John Scott, 'The Bells and the Clock', in Michael Swanton (ed.), *Exeter Cathedral– A Celebration,* (Exeter, 1991), 181-5.
[32] Professor Finberg regarded this as an 'immortal error'. He wrote that John Hooker in 1587 mistook this name and that Monktown refered to an ecclesiastical property in Devon; H.P. R. Finberg, *The Early Charters of Devon and Cornwall* (Occ. Papers No. 2, Leicester, 1953), 4-5.
[33] RAMM, file on the Kelland memorial stone.

POLITICS

The creation of Rougemont Castle by William the Conqueror in 1068 established Exeter as the centre of Crown justice within the county and it has remained so since. In 1537 the city was given the status of a county and was known as the 'city and county of Exeter'. Many of the country's kings and queens have visited the city since then with one exception: Victoria visited Exeter when she was a fourteen-year old princess but as queen only passed through St David's Station. On her first visit in 1833 she remained in her carriage and only stopped outside the London Inn while on the second occasion, in 1856, she did not leave her railway compartment. Exeter was the one of the few cities she failed to officially visit.[34] But it was because of the city's expressed loyalty to the crown that King Henry VII awarded two symbols of his personal regard to Exeter. The city supported the king against the rebel army of Perkin Warbeck in 1497 and the king, on his subsequent visit, gave the right to bear the Cap of Maintenance & Ceremonial Sword which still can be seen in the Guildhall. In 1205 or perhaps even earlier, Exeter was the third city to have a mayor (after London and Winchester). Perhaps, this local pride in its mayoralty explains why in the cathedral there is a stained glass panel portraying one Exeter mayor as a kneeling participant at the Nativity. Has any other English city claimed

The Session House, 1836, in the castle.

---

[34] John Gidley, *Notices of Exeter comprising a history of royal visits,* (Exeter, 1893), 98. Queen Victoria visited Winchester in 1897, stayed in her train compartment and made similar remarks to those she had earlier given at Exeter; information supplied by Winchester City Council.

Left: *The Ancient Cap of Maintenance.*

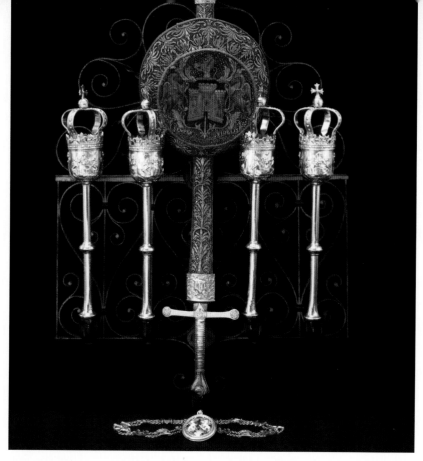

Above: *The Swords hilt.*
Right: *The City's Regalia.*

to have a civic representative at the birth of Christ? And yet there is a long history of not being amused with long-winded politicians: over four hundred years ago, in 1557, a resolution was passed that any councillor who spoke who was 'too tedious, too long or to small effect' was to be fined twelve pence, more than £50 today.[35] The city's guildhall is recognised as the longest serving building of its kind in the country: councillors still debate city business in the fifteenth-century hall but there has been a guildhall on the site since about 1160.[36] It is because of this lineage that the city has the earliest civic seal in the kingdom from about 1200.[37]

---

[35] Hoskins, *Two Thousand Years,* 59.
[36] John Allan, *Exeter Guildhall.*(Exeter, undated), 10.
[37] *English Romanesque Art, 1066–1200* (1984), 319.

A Georgian Civic Procession.

TOURISM

E xeter has long attracted a diverse range of visitors such as a group of native Americans from New England in the early seventeenth century and Pocahontas after them although her thoughts on Exeter were not recorded. In 1688 the nation looked to Exeter when it unwillingly hosted a Dutch invader: William of Orange spent several days here and proclaimed himself king of England. Up until the eighteenth century it was generally however dominated by merchants travelling for commercial purposes, gentry for the quarterly meetings of the county justices and clerics attending diocesan meetings at the cathedral. In the late seventeenth century Exeter had begun to benefit from other men and women travelling en route for Plymouth, then a growing naval port. Then in the middle of the eighteenth century, and continuing until the present time, visitors from throughout the country began to patronise the new seaside resorts along the south, and later north, coasts. A week at Exeter to see the cathedral and partake in the city's cultural life was part of many travellers' itineraries. Later, in the middle of the nineteenth century, Dartmoor was another attraction that brought visitors through the city. Exeter became, and remains, the hub of a tourist culture.

In 1892 Beatrix Potter wrote she was very fond of the city although she deplored the bonfires in front of the cathedral and thought the participants there on the fifth of November were a notorious rabble. Nearly two hundred years before her visit another traveller, a gentleman from Cornwall, thought Exeter was exceptional and regarded the Cathedral Close as 'the very pleasure or jewel of the place'. During Exeter's long years of exceptional prosperity, which lasted until

Left: Georgian Exeter, a view of the High Street with the Guilhall, by John White Abbot, 1797.

39

the middle of the eighteenth century, visitors were greatly impressed by the city. Guides informed travellers of the city's past, not always truthfully, with stories such as how Oliver Cromwell stabled his horses in the cathedral and that the people of Exeter were particularly hostile to Joseph Priestley, the Georgian theologian and man of science who was associated with atheism, and that one local barber, on discovering his client's identity whilst shaving, dropped his razor whilst shouting he had seen Priestley's cloven foot.[38] The number of visitors were catered for by a range of inns and from 1770 by the first hotel in the country. It was that year that Peter Berlon, the French proprietor, advertised his establishment and named it The Hotel. It was later named after the Duchess of Clarence (later wife of William IV) and is now known as the Royal Clarence.[39]

Two thousand years of history have given Exeter a rich and diverse culture. Those elements which have made it the region's capital have also contributed to making it a city distinctive in many ways. Even so, no doubt there is a great deal more to be discovered about the past and even now modern Exeter is fertile ground for future historians to write about.

[38] Gray, *Exeter the Traveller's Tales.* 158, 29, 95, 102.
[39] Hoskins, *Two Thousand Years,* 90.

Illustration Sources
Permission to publish has beeen given by:
Devon Record Office; page 8 *(bottom right)* 18-19, 37.
Exeter City Museums; 4, 10, 11, 13 *(bottom)*, 14, 15, 16, 17, 20, 21,22, 26, 27, 30, 32, 34, 36, 38.
Westcountry Studies Library; 5, 6, 7, 23, 25, 28, 39, 40.
Private Collection; 3, 8 *(left and top)*, 9, 12, 13 *(top)*, 29, 31, 35.
Express and Echo; 24.
Stuart Blaylock. 33.